Dawn of ZOMBIE HAIKU

Ryan Mecum

HOW BOOKS

Cincinnati, Ohio
www.howdesign.com

For more excellent books and resources for designers, visit www.howdesign.com.

15 14 13 12 11   5 4 3 2 1

Distributed in Canada by Fraser Direct, 100 Armstrong Avenue, Georgetown, Ontario, Canada L7G 5S4, Tel: (905) 877-4411. Distributed in the U.K. and Europe by F&W Media International, LTD, Brunel House, Forde Close, Newton Abbot, TQ12 4PU, UK, Tel: (+44) 1626 323200, Fax: (+44) 1626 323319, Email: enquiries@fwmedia.com. Distributed in Australia by Capricorn Link, P.O. Box 704, Windsor, NSW 2756 Australia, Tel: (02) 4577-3555.

Editor: Amy Owen
HOW Books Art Director: Grace Ring
Production Coordinator: Greg Nock

3 1561 00248 2903

Designer/Packager:
Lisa Kuhn/Curio Press, LLC
www.curiopress.com

This journal belongs to

Dawn

D+A
4-ever!

Hello from **NEW YORK CITY**

Hi! My name is Dawn.
I like stickers, cats and books.
This is a haiku.

2

The first and third lines
    each must have five syllables.
Line two has seven.

    Five syllable bread.
    Seven syllable turkey.
    A haiku sandwich!

    I am ten years old.
    I will be eleven soon,
        but soon doesn't count.

    I live with my dad
in our Staten Island home
    in New York City.

Let's get this out now:
I am in love with Andrew!

Glad I got that out.

Writing that haiku
made all my arm hair stand up
and gave me goose bumps.

I love poetry!
    Dad bought me this new journal
    to write thoughts in verse.

Ever since Mom died,
Dad brings me home lots of gifts
to make me happy.

Most presents don't help.
    Dad gets me lots of nice things;
        but none bring back Mom.

I feel less alone
reading the words of poets
who speak to my soul.

Sometimes when I'm bored
I re-write famous poems
into haiku form.

Haiku by Maya Angelou:
Free birds claim the sky.
I know why the caged bird sings.
It sings of freedom.

The bird inside me
fell asleep when my mom died.
Poems wake it up.

7

Mom died years ago,
when I was turning seven.
Her heart stopped working.

My mom is buried
about an hour's drive upstate,
near Sterling Forest.

Dad takes me often
so I can sit by her grave
and read my poems.

When Dad holds my hand
he says that my slender arms
look just like my mom's.

9

I'm a lot like her.
She used to love poems, too—
    unlike her husband.

Dad's a movie buff.
He lets me watch horror films.
    Even rated R!

He drives the ferry
back and forth to Manhattan
    sixteen times a day.

At night when he's done,
we eat dinner on the couch
    and watch DVDs.

If you read this, Dad,
    thanks for this haiku journal.
Get out of my room!

Dad came home early, screaming, "Turn on the TV and pack a small bag!"

Each channel, the news.
On the news, the same story.
The story: Zombies!

We know our zombies.

Thanks to undead cinema,
Dad has me well versed.

Our tastes can differ.
Dad tends to lean Romero,
and I lean more Boyle.

Why would a young girl
watch zombie films with her dad?
Always be prepared!

When news anchors talk,
they try to not say "zombies"—
but describe zombies.

In Kansas City,
the dead have come back to life
and they are hungry.

Same in Chicago,
where they repeat some footage
of a limping man.

Dad is on his cell
screaming to meet at the dock
in one hour from now.

"Is this for real, Dad?!"
He hangs up the phone, kneels down,
and squeezes me tight.

"Fast or slow, Daddy?
Are the zombies fast or slow?"

Calmly, Dad says, "Both."

As I pack my bag,
he updates his Facebook page
with "MEET @ THE DOCK."

I know the answer,
but still ask, "Where will we go?"
Dad yells back, "Statue."

Over many meals,
Dad and I have long discussed
Zombie Escape Plans.

My favorite choice
has always been Alcatraz,
but we live too far.

Dad has always loved
his first Zombie Escape Plan:
Lady Liberty.

"An island nearby...
small, defendable, up high—

and she looks like mom."

But why would we leave
when we live on an island?

"With graveyards," he'd add.

Dad screams up the steps
for me to **hurry it up**
as I pack this book.

I grab a Ziploc
that this journal can fit in,
in case we get wet.

Outside on the street,
people are racing around,
not sure what to do.

We know how this ends.
Zombies will be everywhere
and these guys are screwed.

Our next-door neighbor
is sitting on the sidewalk
crying in his hands.

We try to bring him
along with us to the dock,
but he won't get up.

I run back inside
and pull down from Dad's dresser
the books of Max Brooks.

My dad is confused
until I flash the covers.
Then he understands.

In my neighbor's lap,
I drop the world war Z book
but keep the other.

"Don't worry, Daddy,
I kept the survival guide.
You raised your girl well."

We hear a gun shot,
and we turn around to see
our first walking dead.

He is running fast—
which makes me change preference
of which type I like.

Another gun blast
and the zombie's head explodes...
which makes me feel faint.

Zombies often die
humorously in movies.

This was less funny.

Dad pulls me in close
and then quickly picks me up.
Then he starts to run.

People are screaming
that there is one somewhere near—
which brings more screaming.

We pass a side street
where I see one on her knees
chewing on a thigh.

Everyone looks lost,
so when Dad yells, "Follow me!"

a lot of them do.

We make our way down
to the St. George terminal
and find Dad's ferry.

Standing beside it
is my dad's best friend Michael
and his son, my crush.

I feel faint again
as Andrew runs straight to me
and squeezes me tight.

I say hi to him,
but then I just start to cry,
so he hugs me more.

We have never hugged—
so this is freaking me out
more than the zombies.

25

My dad's friend Michael
points us to his duffel bags
filled up with weapons.

Michael is a guard
(at Zombie Escape Plan B)
on Rikers Island.

Both he and my dad
would talk for hours all night long
planning things like this.

They discuss options
and agree: Escape Plan A
is our best option.

People around us
all start pointing down the street
as we see them come.

Dad shouts out the plan
to anyone listening
    as zombies rush in.

Michael starts shooting
    as Dad picks me up again
and boards the ferry.

Strangers jump on board
    as my dad runs to the helm
        and starts the engine.

I watch a woman
get tackled by a zombie
into the harbor.

A man punches one
whose face is like a pumpkin.
A rotten pumpkin.

A dozen zombies
attempt to get on the boat,
but Michael stops them.

I can't look away
for fear that one might get me,
so I watch them die.

29

A man with a wound
spraying blood like a sprinkler
tries to get on board.

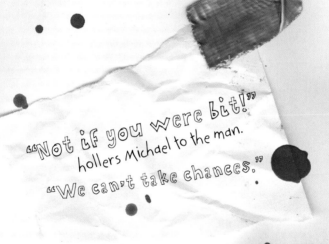

"Not if you were bit!"
hollers Michael to the man.
"We can't take chances."

Andrew holds my hand
as the ferry pulls away
and his dad jumps on.

The bleeding man falls
as arms reach from the water
and pull him under.

A thin blood geyser
gurgles up through the ripples
and then bubbles out.

Dozens of people
gather as Michael explains

the survival plan.

31

In the setting sun,
the Staten Island ferry
heads to the statue.

I should be more scared
but being here with Andrew
makes me feel happy.

And then it hits me.
There are no happy endings in zombie movies.

33

Dad docks the ferry
on Liberty Island's pier,

and Michael steps off.

He tells us to wait.

Half an hour later, he's back
with a few more men.

We get off the boat
and all meet by the flagpole
to discuss what's next.

The island is safe.
There are no zombies on it,
and they have TV. :)

The men will take shifts

watching over the island
with Michael's weapons.

One guarding on foot,
one perched in the statue crown,
and one by the dock.

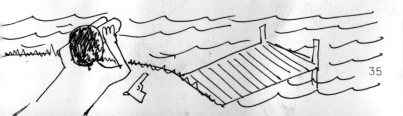

There are some buildings
where we can all take shelter
besides the statue.

Dad picks the gift shop
and he and I make a bed
out of merchandise.

They sell everything.
The Statue of Liberty
looks good on blankets.

Dad puts on my head
a green foam liberty crown
and calls me "Princess."

The group meets again
in the cafeteria
and we cook hot dogs.

Andrew and his dad
are staying in an office
that has Internet.

Andrew invites me
to watch a movie with him
streaming on Netflix.

I have to say no
because Dad doesn't want me
staying up too late.

I still stay up late
watching the news with my dad.

Zombies everywhere.

The streets of L.A.
are filled with thousands of them,
just like Zombieland.

Unlike the movie,
Dad hopes Bill Murray survives

for Ghostbusters 3.

Next they show New York
on videos on YouTube,
which makes us both cry.

We hug each other,
both saying it will be fine...
as our city burns.

Dad mutes the TV

and grabs a gift shop hoodie
to make a pillow.

Michael texts my dad.
He laughs then shows it to me.
"Goodnight, Dawn. —Andrew."

Now Dad is snoring
as I sit here next to him

writing these haiku.

Zombie Haiku by Dylan Thomas
Do not go gentle
into that zombie-plagued night.
And take the shotgun.

Is it still called "dead"
after zombies die again?

Seems like overkill.

Living become dead.
The dead become the undead.
Undead become what?

Is it contagious
or do you have to be bit?
Do ALL dead come back?

Is my mom undead
scratching inside her coffin,
drooling for my brains?

Does a zombie sleep,
and if so, might it have dreams
with past memories?

Is it still my mom
or did her soul fly away
as soon as she died?

If a soul is good
and it goes up to heaven,
are zombies what's left?

Are you in there, Mom?
Was your Zombie Escape Plan
dying beforehand?

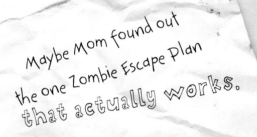

Maybe Mom found out
the one Zombie Escape Plan
that actually works.

I miss you, Mommy.
I hope you didn't come back.
Dad misses you, too.

I like a boy, Mom!

I wish you could have met him.
I hope you still can't.

I'm falling asleep...

or maybe this is a dream

and I'm waking up.

This is not a dream.
The Statue of Liberty
is still above me.

That bed was no good.
I have a kink in my neck—
just like the undead.

The TV is on,
but just like in zombie films,
the cable is out.

I go with my dad
on his zombie guarding shift
up the statue's crown.

Dad tells me to steal
some gift shop binoculars
from the gift shop shelf.

"Give me your tired,
your poor, your huddled masses,
yearning to breathe free."

Lady Liberty

counts "tired" as two syllables.

I'll give it to her.

Can zombies climb steps?
These three hundred, fifty-four
make me feel secure.

A sign on a door
says torch access has been closed
since 1916.

From the Lady's crown,
we can see that everything
is falling apart.

From all the boroughs,
black smoke has blocked out the sun
and ash falls like snow.

49

Zombie Haiku by e.e. cummings

if anyone lived
in this wretched how town (they)
would be soon eaten.

Dad and I brainstorm—
hoping for a happy one—
zombie film endings.

The closest we come
is Night of The Living Dead,
which is still a stretch.

My dad used to say
zombies symbolized something.
Now he thinks they don't.

Dad thinks their decay

mixed with rigor mortis speed
determines their pace.

With binoculars,
Dad sees zombies staring back
from the Jersey coast.

We both are not sure
if the statue looks tasty,
or if they see us.

Along the shoreline,
the undead wade in the bay
and toward our island.

Zombies start to float,

which brings us both some comfort.

Then they start to sink.

We think the same thing:
Along the floor of the bay—

Could they walk to us?!

We race down the steps
to give everyone warning
that we might have guests.

A group of people
are with Michael by the dock,
with binoculars.

Andrew is pointing
way over to Manhattan.
It looks a bit odd.

At Battery Park,
there is a gray cloud of mist
by the water's edge.

Someone is screaming,
"Do dead bodies float or sink?!"

Dad answers back: "Both."

Andrew drops a coin
into pay binoculars
mounted on the fence.

My binoculars
shake hard against my cheek bones,
making things blurry.

Thousands of zombies

are walking off the island
like a waterfall.

Someone else explains,
"They sink when lungs take water.
They rise with gut gas."

Andrew walks over
and says that he'll protect me.
Then he starts to cry.

Dad is frustrated
that his Zombie Escape Plan
missed this one small glitch.

Some people argue,
"Should we get back on the boat
or stay here on land?"

Michael hands out guns
as Hudson River currents
push zombies our way.

The next half hour fills
with frantic shouts and orders
as we get prepared.

Men try to pour gas
around the perimeter,

but the gas runs out.

Women move the food
from the cafeteria

into the statue.

The first one floats past
and although still far away,
he thrashes for us.

A trail of zombies
float like undead lily pads
out into the sea.

For now we are safe
	from any floating zombies—
unless currents change.

The last immigrants
sail past Liberty Island
	like those before them.

			Hundreds of zombies
	form what looks like solid ground.
		I could run across.

		The sound is awful
	as the wet gurgling chorus
	watches us stare back.

Dad says the floaters
are a lot less important
than the ones who sank.

From the Jersey side,
the zombies get much closer
and gunshots explode.

Someone lights the gas,
but it just causes more smoke
and quickly dies out.

The water ripples
as the top of a forehead
cuts like a shark fin.

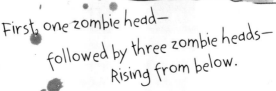

First, one zombie head—
followed by three zombie heads—
Rising from below.

Dad shoots one of them
and someone else shoots two more—
as six more emerge.

Soon, there are dozens
covered in seaweed and sludge
stumbling after us.

Dad curses Max Brooks...
though underwater battles
are warned in his book.

It becomes chaos
      as the first zombie steps foot

   onto the island.

We all start to run.
Dad picks me up and takes us
      back to the gift shop.

Others follow us,
but most run after Michael
      into the statue.

Through the side window,
we watch hundreds of zombies
step out of the bay.

Some run, but most don't.
All heading to the same place...

into the statue.

Dad's cell phone buzzes
and he shows me Michael's text,
    "r u with andrew"

Where could Andrew be?!
            My heart, like hummingbird wings,
            beats fast as I cry.

    They text back and forth
until it is just my dad
        sending unread texts.

            Zombies continue
        to stream into the statue
            as the hours pass by.

A man without legs
drags himself along the shore,

doing endless laps.

It's been a long time
since hearing any gunshots—
which can't be good news.

All of us look up

as we hear screeching metal
from somewhere above.

As Dad starts screaming,
the Statue of Liberty
lets go of her torch.

We watch her arm crash
in the grass in front of us
and bodies bounce out.

Hundreds of zombies
pour out of the statue's base

and run to the arm.

70

My dad is crying
and keeps mouthing the same words,

"They were all in there."

Just like the movies,
the walking dead all huddle
over carcasses.

Suddenly Andrew
races past our gift shop door
and I kill us all.

Before I can think
I have swung the door open
and I let him in.

I go for a hug
but Andrew goes for my neck
and takes out a chunk.

I will soon forget
the look that my dad gives me
as he turns to run.

I fall on the floor
and watch Andrew chase my dad
out onto the lawn.

My heavy breathing

becomes a high-pitched grunting
and then it slows down.

I take a deep breath

and then never let it out

as I pass away.

Zombie Haiku by Emily Dickinson

I heard a fly buzz—
when I became a zombie.
That was one **loud** bug.

I know I am dead.
I don't know HOW I know that,
or know anything.

I think about Mom,
and then Dad, and then Andrew—
who had better **share!**

I have never craved
food I have not yet tasted—
until this moment.

I need to get up,

but it's hard to remember

just how to do that.

I open my mouth

as my neck sprays blood up high,

which sprinkles back down.

All my memories
seem not needed and distant...

except how to **eat**.

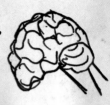

Fear leaves when you die

and is replaced with an urge
to eat somebody.

I quickly stand up
and the realization hits:

I'm a *fast* zombie.

I run to the dock,
watching Andrew and my dad
fighting on the boat.

Dad holds the door shut,
but Andrew and I pulling
flings it wide open.

People used to say
that I have my daddy's eyes.

Well I sure do now.

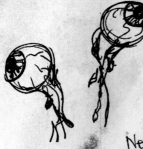

Next I peck his cheek

and then peck and peck some more
'til the cheek is gone.

Zombie Haiku by Sylvia Plath

From head to black shoe,
Daddy, I had to eat you
because I'm starving.

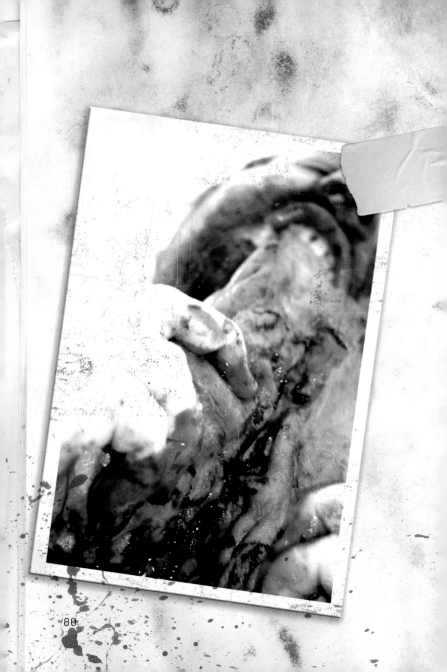

I always liked pork
        but it tastes nothing like Dad—
the other white meat.

Dad used to get mad
when I ate with my fingers,
    so I use my face.

He keeps repeating
        a word that sounds familiar:
    it might be my name.

I've seen Dad shirtless,

so I know where the moles are
        that flavor the flesh.

Daddy hasn't shaved,
so it's rough eating his chin

because it's prickly.

I remember things,
but only stuff that matters.
For example: brains.

My dad stops talking
once we crack open his top
and pull out what's there.

Reaching down Dad's neck
feels like my Christmas stocking.

Who **knows** what's in there?!

Can't find Dad's wishbone,

so Andrew and I make do
with legs and torso.

I vaguely recall
the Humpty Dumpty poem
he would read to me.

It's hard to believe
the organ that creates thought
tastes just like Jell-o.

My throat is clogged up.
I have to use an arm bone
to push down that spleen.

The insides of bones
are filled with a spongy fat

I like to suck out.

No horses or men
would be able to put Dad
together again.

Above my dad's bones,
Andrew stares into my eyes
and pulls me to him.

And then the dead boy
fell in love with the dead girl
gnawing on his neck.

This kink in my neck
has tightened up even worse,
post-rigor mortis.

We run off the boat
over to the statue arm
painted green, with red.

Piles of dark, stained bones
of people I once had met—
I lick for flavor.

We all run around
checking anywhere we can
to find fresh food *first*.

In the rose garden,

zombies tear their flesh on thorns,
releasing air puffs.

Liberty Island
is a plate we have licked clean
and we need more plates.

We stand on the boat,
unable to remember
how to undock it.

Zombie Haiku by Edgar Allen Poe

Right beside the sea
I ate my Annabel Lee.
Quoth the raven, "Brains."

Soon all the zombies
press onto the ferry boat
and it starts to tip.

My haiku journal
stays dry in its plastic bag.
Not so much for me.

Zombies in water
worry less about drowning
than they do starving.

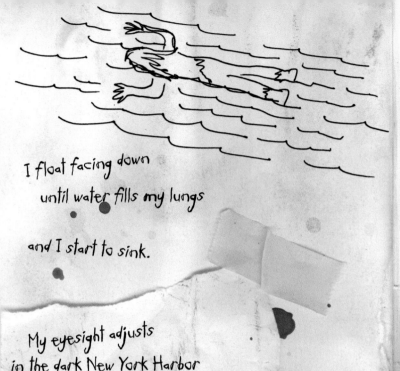

I float facing down
until water fills my lungs

and I start to sink.

My eyesight adjusts
in the dark New York Harbor
to see fins and *teeth*.

Zombie versus shark.
We both stare at each other,
thinking the same thing.

91

The shark bites my hip
as I bite into its gills.
He lets go. I don't.

His enlarged gill hole
allows me to reach inside

and tear at organs.

The shark tries to leave,
but my arm is stuck inside—
so I go with him.

He swims me around
but is quickly losing life
as I keep tearing.

He somehow shakes free,
only to float belly up
as I sink back down.

The current is strong
as I skim along the floor
with other zombies.

Light above brightens,
which leads us back to the world
that was once Brooklyn.

Standing on the beach,
Andrew stares out at the bay
for when I come out.

I stand next to him
and he chews on my neck hole,
which brings him comfort.

Zombie Haiku by William Shakespeare
Shall I compare thee
to a luscious frontal lobe?
If so, thou shall lose.

We start walking north
toward some place I'm longing for,
but I'm not sure why.

Both our heads snap right
after we hear the screaming
and smell the bleeding.

Zombies have smashed through
and are entering a store
filled with what we were.

If, instead of toys,

you got fresh brains for Christmas,
this would be Christmas.

Zombie Haiku by Allen Ginsberg

I saw the best minds
in their degeneration.
Tasty, flavorful.

We all eat for hours,
but sometimes I eat too fast
and lose a knuckle.

Some zombie stomachs
make popping sounds when they burst
like withered balloons.

A zombie pulls veins
that he is still swallowing
from his own chest wound.

The human body
has veins that can stretch for miles.
Limbs stretch three feet, tops.

We all eat so fast,
a pink mist envelops us
like an indoor cloud.

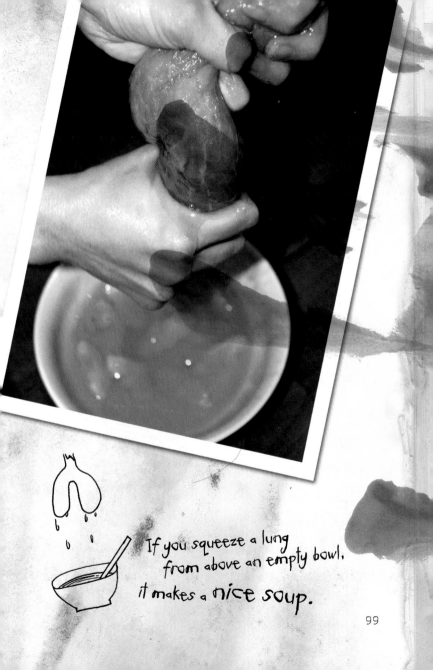

If you squeeze a lung
from above an empty bowl,
it makes a **nice soup.**

I dip my fingers
in fingernail polish blood,

which I just lick off.

As one dead guy eats,
I wait by his stomach hole
for sloppy seconds.

Hair is hard to eat
but it's good wrapped around toes
for added texture.

101

Zombie Haiku by Theodore Roethke

I knew a woman,
in a pile once I ate her,
lovely in her bones.

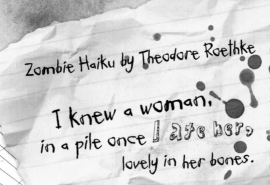

Once the food is gone,
I let instinct steer my feet
and Andrew follows.

We cross Brooklyn Bridge
as wind wisps chunks of our hair
to the East River.

The Manhattan streets
look just like a Zombie Walk
as the zombies walk.

A nearby zombie
dressed head to toe as a clown,
was somebody's dad.

The clown has bite marks
where a zombie stopped eating.
Guess he tastes FUNNY.

My body stiffens.
There's no way "Thriller" zombies

could dance that quickly.

I feel a FLY crawl
deep inside my left nostril—
and then out my mouth.

Zombie Haiku by Shel Silverstein

Where the sidewalk ends,
you can crack a skull open

on the cement edge.

Times Square is still loud,
as all our moaning echoes
off darkened billboards.

I'm chomping on fat
from past overweight victims
like it's chewing gum.

Ash covers Andrew.
The city and his skin now
share the same gray tint.

Clogged Lincoln Tunnel.
It takes days to stumble through,

past car wrecks to light.

Zombie Haiku by T.S. Eliot

We are hollow men.
This is the way the world ends.
Not a bang, but brains.

We are both starving,
so we check nearby houses
for someone **screaming**.

The machete blade
that severs off Andrew's arm
should have surprised us.

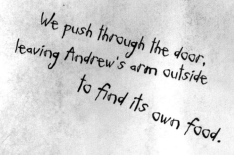

We push through the door,
leaving Andrew's arm outside
to find its own food.

A family fights,
   eventually gives up,
and feeds us dinner.

108

Zombie Haiku by William Shakespeare
To bite through the skull
or beat it against the wall?
That is the question.

Please stop kicking me.
This will be over shortly.

Have an open mind.

Despite all the jokes,
the brains inside blonde women
do seem less meaty.

I used to prefer
face cheeks over other cheeks,
but it all tastes good.

Zombie Haiku by Walt Whitman
Every skin atom
form'd from this soil, this air,
tastes like chicken meat.

You know a meal's good
if it takes about a week
to finish eating.

We head back upstate,
although I have forgotten
why we should go there.

Instinct makes me stop—
while walking past a playground—
to sit on a swing.

Skin as white as snow?
Snow White wasn't a princess

but something more dead.

It was not the kiss
that made Snow White move again,
but his
fresh meat scent.

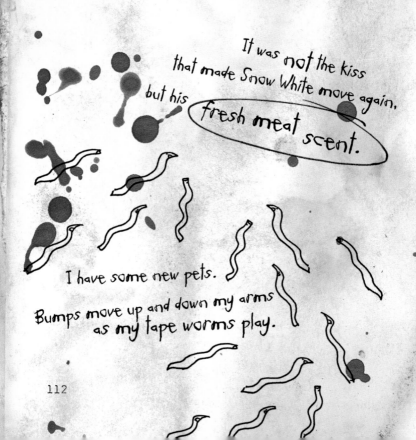

I have some new pets.

Bumps move up and down my arms
as my tape worms play.

I suck out juices
from a chunk of an eyebrow
lodged under my tongue.

The birds in their nests—
as we zombies walk below—
whistle out of tune.

My lips are cracking
so I wipe them in lip balm
I made with thigh fat.

Warm weather turns cold
and all the trees around us

look like they're dead, too.

Zombie in the snow
drags his almost-severed foot,

leaving a red line.

One zombie's feet FROZE in the creek, where he will stand for the next few months.

If I push my eye,
my tear ducts make squishy sounds
and maggots POP Out.

Andrew likes to pick
in his own severed armhole
for something to eat.

On a burning hill,
a young deer carcass gallops.
A fawn of the dead.

Both of us realize
that we are now slow zombies,
as people run past.

It's hard to chase them
with so many rotting bones
not where they should be.

Zombie Haiku by William Butler Yeats

The second coming
is dragging his dead body,
slouching towards warm brains.

We hear a gunshot,
which explains why Andrew's neck
has become see-through.

More zombies join us
and just as quickly leave us
as we lag behind.

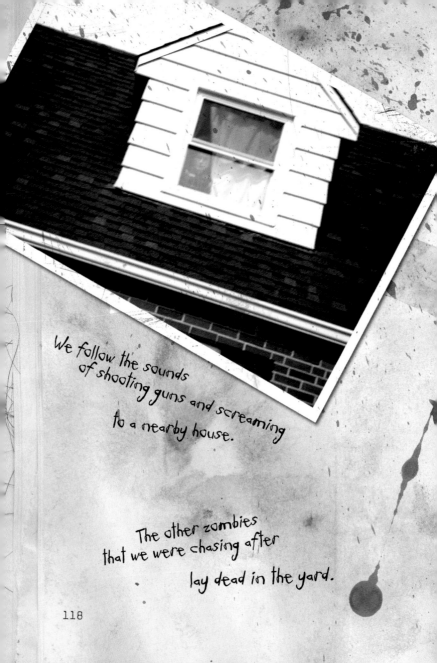

We follow the sounds
of shooting guns and screaming
to a nearby house.

The other zombies
that we were chasing after

lay dead in the yard.

People stare at us
from behind broken windows,
pointing their shotguns.

Since we are slower,
we were able to notice

the man in a tree.

We try to shake it
as he tries to shoot at us.
And then a limb snaps.

119

People from the house
fire guns at us from afar
as we chase the man.

He has a limp, too,
so he kind of looks like us
as he tries to run.

We slowly catch up
as he hobbles through the woods
and drops his shotgun.

He trips in a creek,
which makes his wet skin SQUEAKY

when I gnaw on it.

121

Swallowing is hard.

His trachea keeps sticking

in mY trachea.

That hanging throat thing,
your tonsil or uvula,
is fun to chew through.

Zombie Haiku by Robert Frost
Two lungs in the chest.
I eat the bloodier one—
not much difference.

When Andrew eats now,
he shoves meat in his neck hole,
which saves chewing time.

We roam through the woods
as nearby zombie chipmunks
feast on squeaking ones.

Sometimes, when I'm bored,
I pull tapeworms from arm holes
and push them back in.

I groan with clenched teeth
but moan with an open mouth.
There's a difference.

As night approaches,
Andrew tries holding my hand
but snaps off his thumb.

Bloody cheeks glisten,
and his hair whispies glow white
under the moonlight.

He stares in mY eyes

as I pull his head to mine
while gently moaning.

It looks like kissing
as we search each other's mouths
for unswallowed brain.

125

So many flavors—
salty, grainy and moldy—
hide inside his face.

His moans seem to say,
"Though your beauty will decay,
your brains will stay sweet."

Zombie Haiku
by Elizabeth Barrett Browning

How do I love thee?
Since all my fingers fell off
I can't count the ways.

Beauty is skin deep
and beauty tastes really good—

so I'm lipless now.

We hold each other
until the sun rises up
and we walk again.

127

A lost memory
of maybe missing something

makes me feel lonely.

We walk down a road
that somehow seems familiar

after every turn.

Our decayed bodies
are quickly falling apart
so sometimes we crawl.

Shouting behind us
gives us enough energy
to slowly stand up.

A man with a gun
fires it many times at us

as we reach for him.

Now out of bullets,
he runs away up the street,

as Andrew falls down.

129

"Look inside your heart
and see if you still love me.
look through your chest hole."

I can see pavement through numerous body holes—
including his head.

His skull splits open
into the shape of a heart
and I salivate.

From my shirt pocket
drops the moldy Max Brooks book
that didn't save him.

Although long rotten,
I taste what was once his brain
because it seems right.

Zombie Haiku by e.e. cummings
i carry your brain
(i carry it in my gut)
next to both our hearts

I know I am close,
so I leave Andrew behind
and keep walking on.

Covered in green moss,
the Sterling Cemetery
is at the road's end.

I lean through the gate,
and although I don't know why,
I know where to go.

133

I walk through the rows
and past dozens of gravestones
to kneel at one plot.

My hands are broken
but still I force them to dig
into the damp earth.

DaY turns into night
as I continue to scrape
until I collapse.

134

Somewhere under me,
I hear the sounds of digging...
even when I stop.

I no longer sleep
but since my body is weak
it looks like I do.

Spurts of energy
slowly help me continue
moving dirt around.

135

Another zombie
watches me for a few days
and then walks away.

One hand is now gone,
but the wristbone in its place
makes a nice shovel.

Though digging for days,
I have barely dug a foot
below the grass roots.

Voices behind me
cause me to thrust more quickly
down into the soil.

People holding guns
and heavy tools as weapons
watch me scrape the ground.

I moan as I dig,

and something deep below me

mournfully moans back.

Somebody kicks me
and I roll to a gravestone
that somehow I know.

Once upon a time,
I had a sheet of paper
and a pink crayon.

Somebody and I
scratched out a gravestone rubbing
against this etched rock.

Up from below me
the bones from a slender arm
reach out from the dirt.

A body climbs out
and wraps its arms around me
as a gun goes off.

I can't remember...
but then suddenly I do
and I squeeze her back.

A few more gunshots
give me a happy ending
in my mother's
arms.

About the Design

Dawn of Zombie Haiku is designed by Lisa Kuhn, owner of Curio Press, located in Cincinnati, Ohio. Curio Press is devoted to high quality book design and packaging. For more information visit: www.curiopress.com

About the Author

Ryan Mecum's Zombie Escape Plan is one he stole from Max Brooks. Once the dead come back, Ryan intends to transport his family to an offshore oil rig, where they will live off of seafood and wear chain mail shark suits and brain-protecting helmets for the rest of their lives. This is Ryan's fourth book in his Horror Haiku series. He also wrote Zombie Haiku, Vampire Haiku, and Werewolf Haiku. He graduated with a degree in English Literature from the University of Cincinnati and lives in Cincinnati with his family. You can find more information about him at www.ryanmecum.com.

This one's for my kids:
When I go, if I come back,
aim for Daddy's head.

Also Check Out

ZOMBIE HAIKU, VAMPIRE HAIKU + WEREWOLF HAIKU
by Ryan Mecum

Find these books and many others at MyDesignShop.com or your local bookstore.